D1628791

MY FAMILY, YOUR FAMILY

MY FAMILY, YOUR FAMILY

Richard Leighton

gatekeeper press™

Columbus, Ohio

MY FAMILY, YOUR FAMILY

Published by Gatekeeper Press
2167 Stringtown Rd, Suite 109
Columbus, OH 43123-2989
www.GatekeeperPress.com

The editorial work for this book is entirely the product of the author. Gatekeeper Press did not participate in and is not responsible for any aspect of this element.

Library of Congress Control Number: 2022951300

ISBN (hardcover): 9781662932854

ACKNOWLEDGEMENTS

I am indebted to three family members who supplied much of the information and photographs that pertained to their family branches.

They are my nephew, **Vernon Leighton** and my two nieces **Cathy Boulter** and **Diane Moore.**

Vernon Leighton

Cathy Boulter

Diane Moore

PROLOGUE

I am writing this book to preserve a family history for my descendants and the descendants of my brother, hence the name " My Family, Your Family." The book is intended to preserve this history in pictures as well as in words. Photographs can be saved in albums, of course, but I find photo albums a bit large and unwieldy. Then, too, a photo album can be kept by one family or person whereas a published book can be the possession of many individuals.

I've begun with the great grandparents those of mine and my brother's and of our wives, Frances and Dottie. Even though we never knew our great grandparents, I have photographs and some information about them that should be of interest to our descendants.

A more remote history of the Leightons and the Vernons may be found in the books of Helene Staley (1,2) and the more remote Cale family history in Janice Cale Sisler's book (3) but as far as I know, there are no publications that relate the history of the Houcks, Schars, Scaggs. Murphys, Brocks or Chapins.

CHAPTER 1
Great Grandparents: The Leightons & Vernons

Isaac Leighton

Isaac Leighton was born May 21, 1828 in Stourbridge, Worcestershire, England. At the age of 13, like his father **Richard,** he began working as a puddler or forge man in the Iron Works of Stourbridge. In 1849, at the age of 21 he married **Elizabeth Vernon**, daughter of **Joseph Vernon** and **Elizabeth Frith. Joseph Vernon** had multiple jobs. He was a tailor, draper and postmaster and agent of the District Fire Assurance Office. At the time of their marriage **Elizabeth Vernon** was 17 years old, having been born June 3, 1832.

The Vernon name is prominent in English folklore. spelled out in Charles Major's novel (4) about the elopement of the famously beautiful **Dorothy Vernon** and **John Manners** who then inherited Haddon Hall in Derbyshire, England, the estate of Dorothy's father, **Sir George Vernon**. Later a film based on the novel starred Mary Pickford. Haddon Hall remains in the Manners family to this day. Just how **Elizabeth Vernon** and her father, **Joseph**, may have been related to **Sir George** and **Dorothy Vernon** is unclear but we can speculate that they may have been descendants.

Elizabeth Vernon Leighton

After the marriage **Isaac** and **Elizabeth** lived with her widowed father for two years before emigrating to America in 1851. They sailed from Liverpool that year and first settled in New York. It's not clear what motivated this move. It may be that he and his father-in-law didn't get along well since it is said that the Vernons didn't approve of this marriage; or perhaps after 10 years as a puddler, **Isaac** wanted a change in occupation. Puddlers still worked in this country, changing wrought iron to pig iron in crude furnaces. An historic marker may be found along the road near Uniontown, Pennsylvania, honoring the first puddlers in America.

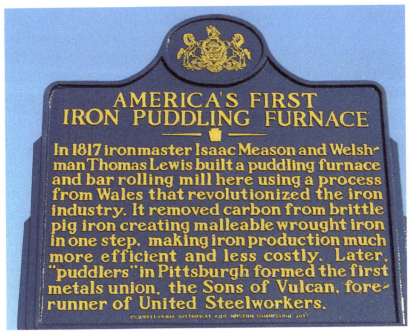

Puddler Marker

It may be that **Isaac** continued working as a puddler after the immigration but if so, he soon gave it up to pursue farming.

In their early American years the lives of **Isaac** and **Elizabeth** were marked by multiple moves and the births of children. First they lived in Sloatsburg, New York, then Trenton, New Jersey, Mt. Savage, Maryland and Chestnut Ridge, West Virginia. In between these addresses they apparently lived in Pennsylvania and Ohio. All told, they had 11 children, three of whom died in childhood. Their ninth child was my grandfather, **Herbert Vernon Leighton.**

Isaac's most successful farm was the last one, in Chestnut Ridge, West Virginia. He was a religious man and a musician. While I don't know what instruments he played, I know that for many years he devoted his spare time to teaching instrumental and vocal music. He had a strong singing voice and in his later years he was known for his Gospel singing. A faithful member of the Methodist Episcopal Church, for over 20 years he was a Sunday School Superintendant and class leader.

Isaac and **Elizabeth** both died in 1911, he on January 4th and she on March 31st. Apparently in their later years Isaac and Elizabeth didn't live together since he died in Loch Lynn, in the house of his son, Herbert Vernon and she died in Terra Alta, West Virginia, in the home of her daughter, Minnie. Isaac and Elizabeth are buried in the Oakland Cemetery with their daughters Ada and Rhoda, all in the same plot.

CHAPTER 2
Great Grandparents:
The Cales

Unique among the great grandparents are the Cales. Not immigrants, they descended from several generations going back to Christopher Cale who came to this country in the late 18th century, perhaps as a Hessian soldier in the Revolutionary War, as I've proposed in my novel about his life (5).

Henry Edgar Cale was my great grandfather, the son of **Jacob Cale, Jr.** who was the grandson of Christopher.

Henry Cale was born February 18, 1836 in West Virginia. Henry managed a 100 acre farm near Bruceton Mills, West Virginia. He married twice and fathered 10 children, all of whom survived childhood. His first wife was **Sarah Elizabeth Feather,** daughter of **Joseph B. Feather** and **Lydia Hartman Feather.** She was the mother of seven of the 10 children including my grandmother, **Mary Maude Cale Leighton.**

In addition to his farming chores, **Henry** was postmaster in Bruceton and kept a general store there. He also served as Secretary of the Preston County District School Board. A restless soul, at times he lived in nearby Elliottville, Pennsylvania. In his mid-thirties Henry ventured into the field of proprietary medicine. With William Albright he sponsored advertisements in the Preston County Journal for Fahrney's Blood Cleanser or Panacea. This root and herbal concoction was sold by Dr. Peter Fahrney of Chicago, a formula he inherited from his grandfather. The medicine was said to give one "a sense of vitality," perhaps because it contained 14% alcohol. **Henry** may have been a member of the Brethren Church because Fahrney's network of sponsors and consumers extended throughout the Brethren.

Henry & Sarah Cale

Henry also took subscriptions for the Preston County Journal. Henry died April 29, 1905 and is buried in Sugar Valley Cemetery near Bruceton Mills, West Virginia.

Henry Cale's headstone

CHAPTER 3
Great Grandparents: The Houcks

The family of **Michael** and **Charlotte Haug** (later changed to Houck) embarked on an 85 day voyage across the Atlantic in 1854. Michael had been recruited from his home in Wurttemberg, Darmstat, Germany by the Whitney Glass Works. Seven of the eight Haug children survived the voyage, including my great grandfather, **William John (or Johann).** At the time of this immigration he was nine years old, having been born in 1845.

William Johann Houck

The family landed in Castle Garden, New Jersey and quickly settled in Glassboro, living in a house that belonged to the Whitney Glass Works and they shopped in the company store. The Whitney company closed its doors in 1895 and was purchased by Owens Illinois, the company that eventually employed my grandfather.

A religious family, the Houcks were instrumental in founding the German Reformed Church at the Triangle, so called because of its location at the intersection of Main and Union Streets. Certainly they felt at home there since all the services were conducted in the German language. This practice continued until 1917 when they changed to English services, perhaps to avoid the recrimination that they were enemies of this country in World War I.

William Johann Houck became a blacksmith and had a shop on Delsea Drive in Glassboro. He married **Mary C. Dischert** who was 23 years younger than he. Mary's father, **Justus Dischert** was another founding member of the German Reformed Church.

Mary Dischert Houck

William and **Mary** had five children. The oldest was **Frederick Phillip**, my grandfather. Three other children survived childhood. Two of them are shown in this family picture. The boys' sister, **Amalia,** ("Millie") is not shown.

Left to right: Mary, Jacob, Harry and William Houck

In 1868 **William** and **Mary** gave up the blacksmith shop and moved to Camden where **William** opened a saloon. The saloon became quite profitable and at the urging of his customers, **William** began investing his money in horse racing at a track located in Gloucester, New Jersey. He became addicted to this sport and soon lost almost all the money he had accumulated.

In 1896 **William** left his saloon and his fixation on the race track, moved back to Glassboro and worked in a furniture store. In the next few years he and **Mary** made multiple moves, all within Glassboro.

Unfortunately, **William** began drinking heavily and died of tuberculosis at the age of fifty nine. At that time, in 1904, before the advent of anti-tubercular drugs, tuberculosis was a common infection.

It was usually contracted at an early age and then became re-activated when an individual was in a debilitated or immune compromised state, as William probably was with his alcoholism.

Mary moved in with her son **Jacob** and his wife but she became very despondent and attempted to take her own life. After that incident she had to be committed to Lakeland Mental Hospital where, at age 48 she also died of tuberculosis.

CHAPTER 4
Great Grandparents: The Schars

Benedict or Benjamin Schar was born July 4, 1819 in Zimlisberg in the Bern Canton of Switzerland. His parents were **Samuel** and **Maria Gosteli Schar.** In 1849 at the age of 30 he emigrated to this country. He came by sailboat, landing in New York City. From there he went by train to Sewickley, Pennsylvania where he was hired as a gardener by two rich elderly ladies. One of them was named Mrs. Kirher. These women taught him English and paid him well. After three years he had saved enough money to send for his parents and his oldest brother, Sam and his wife and child.

Subsequently **Benedict** married **Margaret Holl** (also spelled Holle). He and **Margaret** settled in Tarentum, Pennsylvania where he managed a farm.

Benedict Schar

Benedict and **Margaret** had six children. The youngest, born in 1867 was **Anna,** my grandmother. The Schars liked to have family reunions.

Schar Reunion, 1901

This photo depicts the Schar reunion, held in 1901. In this picture **Benedict** appears, sitting in a chair in the center of the second row. My grandmother, **Anna Schar Houck** is second from the right in that row and my mother, **Leona Houck** is second from the right in the first row.

Benedict Schar died in 1932 and was buried in Highland Presbyterian Cemetery, Allegheny County, Pennsylvania.

CHAPTER 5
Great Grandparents:
The Brocks and Chenerys

Alvan Dinsmore Brock was born September 15, 1830 in Buckfield, Maine. He married **Martha Chenery** of Massachusetts. Martha was born in August of 1832. They had two sons, one of whom was **Fenelon Brock.** Alvan became a small town newspaper owner and editor in Maine. Even as a youth he founded the Portland Courier.

He became involved in other newspapers where he was a writer and editor, including the North Adams Sentinel, North Adams, Massachusetts. He also represented that newspaper at editors' conventions.

Later, as editor of the Bangor Whig, he aided the cause of the Abolitionist Party, of which he was an ardent member. When the Civil War broke out, he organized a company of soldiers that he led as their Captain. He was cited for gallantry when Union forces attacked Fort Mahone, Petersburg, Virginia. In that battle, over half of the soldiers in his company died.

After the war he was one of the original members of the Soldiers and Sailors' Union and was a delegate to the convention held by the Union to secure the nomination of General Grant for President. He became managing editor of the Washington Chronicle. In that position, he became interested in the efforts of Miss Clara Barton to identify the graves of Union soldiers who died in Confederate prison camps.

Captain Alvan D. Brock

His wife, Martha died on February 19, 1875 at the early age of 43.

Leaving the newspaper business, **Alvan** worked for the Federal government. First he was an Examiner in the Patent Office but his longest Federal job was in the Government Printing Office where he served as foreman in the Specification Room and later as foreman in the Job Room. In those positions he was largely instrumental in securing Senate passage of the eight-hour workday for workers in the Government Printing Office.

The Federal government in postbellum America was highly partisan, with the Republicans resisting the efforts of the resurgent, pro-Southern Democrats to dismantle Reconstruction. The Public Printer of the United States, Alvan's boss, Mr. Rounds, was an ardent Republican. He asked Alvan, while collecting his salary, to spend two weeks in New York City, convincing typesetters at the New York Tribune to end their strike so the newspaper could endorse the Republican, James G. Blaine for President. Alvan failed to persuade the workers. Subsequently Blaine lost the election to Grover Cleveland. The Democrats in Congress accused both Rounds and Brock of corruption and they both lost their jobs.

Alvan Brock's later life was marked by his inclusion in failed utopian projects. First he got involved in a project to build a railroad from St. Louis to the Mexican terminus port in Topolobampo. A utopian community without private property was planned as part of the project. The scheme ended because of rising costs and disease: malaria and smallpox.

Alvan left this project and moved to Los Angeles where he set himself up as a real estate agent, remarried and planned another utopian community. He and his new wife moved to San Francisco where they became members of a Nationalist Club and an Altrurian Council: organizations devoted to socialist causes. The Brocks joined a group that was building a utopian commune called Altruria near Berkeley, California. Another failed project: the land couldn't support the number of people in the group.

In addition to his involvement in socialist causes, Alvan was interested in science. He obtained a patent for a coiled boiler for steam. He wrote articles in magazines promoting electric technology. Supported by a government pension for Northern soldiers of the Civil War, Alvan Brock eventually suffered dementia and was admitted to the Old Soldiers Home in Hampton, Virginia. From there, in his demented state, he wandered into the streets and was killed by a streetcar on February 20, 1900.

CHAPTER 6
Great Grandparents: The Chapins

Sobieski Loander Chapin was born on October 10, 1837. The Chapins were an old Puritan family, descendants of **Samuel Chapin** who migrated to New England in the 1630s. A deacon and magistrate, Samuel's statue still stands in Springfield, Massachusetts.

Samuel Chapin's statue

One branch of the Chapin family, including Sobieski's father, settled along the border between Pennsylvania and New York, near Ulysses, Pennsylvania. **Sobieski** served in the Civil War on the Union side, as a guard of prisoners.

After the Civil War **Sobieski** married **Sarah Eliza Lawrence** who was born on February 8,1860. They moved to Virginia where he owned and farmed a portion of the land where the battle of Bull Run had been fought. That land is now part of Dulles International Airport. Sobieski and Sarah were the parents of **Alvin Willett Chapin. Alvin** was born on December 2, 1860. Sarah died on May 8, 1916 and **Sobieski** died on June 5, 1918.

CHAPTER 7
Great Grandparents: The Scaggs, Hines and Murphys

Charles Albert Scaggs was the grandson of **Alfred Scaggs** who emigrated to this country from England in the 1820s, first settling in Virginia before he bought land in Howard County, Maryland that he parceled among his eight children.

Charles Albert was born in Wheeling, West Virginia on July 19, 1857. As a young man he moved to Howard County where he farmed one of the sites that his father had inherited from **Alfred Scaggs**.

Charles Albert Scaggs married **Martha Leishear** who was born in 1859. His uncle Isaac established a grocery store with a post office in the store. With this postal address, the town of Scaggsville, Maryland was established. The store and post office were located at the intersection of Scaggsville Road (Route 216) and Old Columbia Road. Scaggsville was a stopping off place for travelers from Baltimore to Washington. The post office lasted until 1952 when Route 29 was paved and the store was torn down.

Charles Albert was the father of **Arthur Scaggs. Charles** had a long life. He outlived his wife by 47 years. She died in 1898. **Charles** had a tragic and untimely death in 1945 when he was run over by a truck in Washington, D.C.

John Hamilton Hines was born on July 1, 1864. He married **Mary Emma Murphy** who was born July 25, 1867 at Fulton, Maryland. **John** and **Mary Emma** were the parents of **Bessie Lurean Hines Scaggs. Mary Emma** died at home in Scaggs- ville on April 19, 1929 and **John** died on April 17, 1942.

Benjamin Franklin Murphy was born on August 18, 1854. He married **Ida Eugenia Souder** on February 14, 1884. They had seven children, including **Elsie May Murphy.**

Benjamin and Ida Murphy

Benjamin died on November 20, 1933 and Ida died on January 18, 1944. As far as I can determine, Benjamin and his descen- dants are not related to George or Mary Emma Murphy so the Scaggs descendants have Murphy ancestors on both sides of their family.

CHAPTER 8
Grandparents: The Leightons and Cales

Herbert Vernon Leighton, the son of Isaac Leighton and Elizabeth Vernon Leighton, was born in Chestnut Ridge, Preston County, West Virginia on October 15, 1870. He and Mary Maude Cale were married on October 14, 1897.

Young Herbert Vernon Leighton

Mary Maude Cale, the daughter of **Henry Cale** and **Sarah Feather Cale** was born January 28, 1874.

Young Mary Maude Cale

Young Herbert Vernon and Mary Maude Cale Leighton)

Initially **Herbert Vernon** and **Mary Maude Leighton** lived in Swanton, Maryland. It was there that my father, **Herbert Cale Leighton** was born on March 22, 1899.

Young Herbert Cale Leighton

Herbert Vernon Leighton had several occupations. Living in Swanton, Maryland for one year he taught school in Oakland, Maryland. He traveled to Oakland on horseback, a distance of 11 miles. The attendance and pay were meager so the next year he moved to Loch Lynn, a suburb of Mt. Lake Park, Maryland. First he owned a general store and afterwards a sawmill in Loch Lynn.

My father grew up in Loch Lynn where the younger Leighton children, all girls, were born. The oldest girl, **Sara Elizabeth,** was later called Betty. Her sisters were **Margaret Frith** and **Mary Helen,** known as Helen.

Left to right, 1ˢᵗ row: Herbert V., Baby Helen, Mary M., Margaret. 2ⁿᵈ row: Herbert C. and Elizabeth

Herbert Vernon Leighton was a very welcoming man who took on the role of head of the household. In his final years, his father, **Isaac** lived with him and his widowed sister **Rhoda** lived there until she died in 1939. Likewise his wife's spinster sister, **Blanche** became a member of the Leighton household until she died in 1950.

His daughter, **Elizabeth** married Laurel Stephenson. They had two children: **Barbara** and **Edward Stephenson.** After she became widowed in 1939, she completed a masters degree in chemistry at the University of Maryland, then moved to New York City to work for the General Foods Corporation. **Barbara** and **Edward** moved in with and were raised by their grandparents and their Great Aunt **Blanche.** Subsequently **Elizabeth** married Glenn Randol.

Margaret Leighton married William Day Mullinix and they became school teachers. **Helen** married Howard Nelson Carmichael who became an executive with a shoe company in Nashville, Tennessee.

When I was old enough to have a bicycle, I would bike from my home in Oakland to visit with my cousin, **Eddie** at our grandparents' house in Loch Lynn. On festive occasions like Thanksgiving and Christmas the extended family would gather at this house for large dinners. There had been a clay tennis court on the grandparents' property, next to the garage but during my childhood years it had fallen in disrepair. Fortunately, well kept tennis courts were available in nearby Mt. Lake Park.

Soon after we moved to Oakland, my dad and granddad constructed a lumber mill that was part hardware store. It was located behind the funeral home.

H.V. Leighton continued working in the lumber mill until his death on October 27, 1946. At that time **Barbara** had left for college and **Edward** enrolled in the Mercersburg Academy, Mercersburg PA where he completed his high school years.

Herbert Cale and Herbert Vernon Leighton
in the lumber mill

After **H.V.'s** death his wife, **Mary Maude** continued to live in their house in Loch Lynn, joined in her later years by her daughter, **Elizabeth** and Glenn Randol. **Mary Maude Cale Leighton** had a long life, enabling her to enjoy her great grandchildren. She died on November 3, 1973 at the age of 99.

Left to right: Barbara, Cathy, Kim and Mary Maude Leighton

CHAPTER 9
Grandparents:
The Houcks and Schars

My grandfather, **Frederick Phillip Houck,** was born in Glassboro, New Jersey on November 18, 1868. His father was **William Johann Houck** and his mother was **Mary Dischert Houck.** My grandfather was the oldest of four children, born into a dysfunctional family. As a result, he had to take on adult responsibilities even in childhood.

In his teenage years he started out to be a blacksmith like his father but he changed to enter the glass industry like his grandfather. He worked for the Whitney Glass Works, serving an apprenticeship as a mold maker. With this early start, he wasn't able to complete a high school education. He did manage to attend a German Lutheran Church school where he learned to read and speak German.

As a young man he moved to Tarentum, Pennsylvania to work for the Flaccus Glass Company. In Tarentum he took his meals at a boarding house that was run by **Anna Schar** (born May 18, 1868) and her three sisters. Apparently she won Fred's heart through his stomach because they soon became engaged and were married on August 23, 1893.

Young Anna and Fred Houck

Fred and Anna had five children, four of whom survived to adulthood.

Their son Howell died at age five from measles related pneumonia.

In those early years **Fred** moved frequently, working as a mold maker in different glass companies. First they moved back to Glassboro, then to Streater, Illinois where my mother, **Leona Ronelva** was born. With the enlarging family, life was difficult for the Houcks in Streator. At one point Fred had to pawn his watch to buy flour so they would have bread to eat. While the family remained in Streator, Fred left to work at a glass company in Marion, Indiana.

Next they moved to Camden, New Jersey and **Fred** worked there as well as in Philadelphia. From Camden the family moved to Bellaire, Ohio where **Fred** worked at the Bellaire

Bottle Company and the Rodefer Glass Company. While in Bellaire, Fred's sister, **Amelia** or **"Millie"** came to live with the Houck family while she worked as a clerk in a department store in nearby Wheeling, West Virginia. She became well known to the Houck children's playmates in Bellaire and they all referred to her as "Aunt Millie." Eventually she married a businessman from New Jersey named Clarence Davis and she moved away.

*Left to right, 1ˢᵗ row: Fritz, Howell and Leona Houck.
2ⁿᵈ row: Myrdith and Earl Houck*

With the family established in Bellaire, **Fred** continued to work at other glass plants in the Northeast. At those times he and Anna would exchange letters. It's interesting to read several of these letters that have been preserved by **Vernon Leighton.** Fred's letters began with "Dear Mother" and Anna's with "Dear Dad." A major topic was laundry: dirty laundry that **Fred** sent her to wash and clean laundry that she sent back. She was always concerned with his appearance, worried that he wasn't sending the laundry in a timely fashion.

The letters also showed concern for their son, **Earl,** who, during World War I was a medical corpsman in France. Following Earl's safe return and enrollment in the University of Pennsylvania, there's a letter from him which indicates he was on the laundry circuit as well.

After 15 years in Bellaire the family made their final move: to Fairmont, West Virginia where **Fred** was invited by Michael Owens (the inventor of the automatic bottle machine) to organize the mold shop into a union of the American Flint Glass Workers Union. As a result, **Fred** became the corresponding secretary for his local labor union. As a union representative, he attended many conferences that were frequently held in Atlantic City. He was proud of his work in smoothing over differences and settling disputes peacefully.

The Houck home sat on a hilltop in the Homewood Addition of Fairmont. It became a centerpiece for the family, located midway between the houses of their son, **Frederick (Fritz)** and their daughter, **Myrdith.** Then daughter **Margaret (Peg)** and her husband, Jim Hinebaugh had a house built across the street from **Fred** and **Anna.**

Fred's household was one of the last houses on the street to get an electric refrigerator. I remember the icebox refrigerator located in a covered porch outside the kitchen that was replenished with twice weekly ice deliveries.

Since **Fred** never owned a car and didn't know how to drive, he hiked up and down this hill daily to get to the streetcar line at the bottom of the hill. Even in his eighties he could climb the hill faster than men and boys much younger than he.

As a child and teenager, I loved my visits there since I could be pampered by multiple family members while visiting my cousins.

Playing marbles was a favorite pastime and Granddad **Fred** would supply my brother and me with glass marbles of various colors, courtesy of Owens-Illinois. For my mother he had gifts of imported German paring knives.

Fred was a proud member of the Prohibition Party and he voted for their candidates in every election. Much of his prohibition zeal was probably a result of his father's alcoholism. Evidently his attitude was passed on to his children. I know there was never any alcohol in our house.

Fred was edentulous and preferred to stay that way. He was aided in this choice by **Anna** who made sure solid food was chopped up before he encountered it. Later in life his son-in-law, Harry Layman who operated a dental laboratory, made a set of dentures for him. After 20 years of being toothless, **Fred** couldn't adjust to a mouthful of teeth. In addition, they interfered with his desire to chew tobacco, perhaps his only vice.

From his base with Owens-Illinois in Fairmont, **Fred** continued to work at other sites: Coshocton, Ohio, Jeanette, Pennsylvania and Charleston, West Virginia.

Forced to retire at the age of eighty, **Fred** continued to work as a night watchman at Owens-Illinois. He was honored for many years as the oldest living annuitant in O-I's Service Retirement Plan. He continued to visit the Owens plant on daily walks into his nineties.

Retired Fred Houck

Anna Schar Houck lived to the age of eighty five and died on May 13, 1954. With Anna's death **Fred** moved into Myrdith's house since Myrdith's husband, Harry had died and **Myrdith** was able to take care of **Fred** in his last years.

Anna Houck

A lifelong Mason, **Fred** served his lodge in all capacities. In 1961 he was honored by his Bellaire Lodge as a Knight of the York Cross of Honor, the highest honorary degree in the York Rite of Freemasonry.

The degree is conferred only on those who have held the highest office in each of the four bodies of the rite.

Fred Houck as a Mason

Fred died at Myrdith's home on June 4, 1964.

CHAPTER 10
Grandparents:
The Brocks and Burritts

Fenelon Barker Brock, the son of **Alvan Dinsmore Brock** and **Martha Chenerey,** was born on August 15, 1858.

Fenelon Brock

He married **Lillian Burritt** who was born on February 18, 1858 in Herrick, Pennsylvania.

Lillian Burritt Brock

Lillian was the daughter of **Samuel Burritt** and **Amanda Nichols Burritt**. Samuel lived from 1808 to 1863.

Fenelon and **Lillian Burritt Brock** had five children: a son named **Walter Brock** and four daughters: **Lillian, Esther, Ann Marian and Dorothy Fenelon Brock.** Their father, **Fenelon** was a patent attorney who had a dozen patents of his own. **Lillian Burritt Brock** died on August 20, 1931 in Washington, D.C. and **Fenelon** died on September 4,1933.

Alvin Willett Chapin married **Grace Raymond Lewis.** They were the parents of **Mabel Louise Chapin. Alvin Chapin** became a wealthy store owner in Washington, D.C.

Alvin Willett Chapin

Grace Raymond Lewis Chapin

The Chapins frequently spent their summers in Chautauqua, New York. **Grace** was well educated. She enjoyed painting landscapes around Chautauqua.

Anthaneum Hotel, Chautauqua, NY

CHAPTER 11
Grandparents: The Scaggs, Hines, Connells and Murphys

Arthur Scaggs, Fran's grandfather, was born on September 16, 1881. He married **Bessie Laureen Hines.** The daughter of **John Hamiton** and **Mary Emma Hines, Bessie** was born on January 16, 1888. **Arthur** and **Bessie** had two children: **Melvin** and **Elsie.** The Scaggs family lived in Scaggsville, next door to the Methodist Church where they were faithful members. In his later years **Arthur** was incapacitated by crippling arthritis. He died on December 28, 1949 and **Bessie** died in June of 1961.

Left to Right: Georgia, Elsie, Bessie, Melvin, Arthur and Will Scaggs

One of six children, **James William Connell** was born on November 23, 1886.

Last row, left to right: Alice, James, Ernest, Brice and Annie Connell. Seated: The Connell's mother. In front: Florence Connell

On January 11, 1911 he married **Elsie May Murphy** who was born on September 13, 1889. The daughter of **Benjamin** and **Ida Murphy,** she was also one of five children.

Young James and Elsie Connell

James or Jim worked as a delivery man, transporting groceries and ice from Laurel to nearby Scaggsville and other communities in Howard County. In his younger years he drove a horse and wagon and later a pickup truck.

Left to right: Brice and James Connell, Alice Wren, Ernest Connell and Florence Marlow

Elsie was an active member of Emmanuel Methodist Church in Scaggsville and was a charter member of the Women's Society of Christian Service. In her later years **Elsie** suffered from dementia. She preceded **James** in death, passing away on August 22, 1962 while **James** died on October 8, 1965.

3rd from Left: Elsie Connell with siblings

CHAPTER 12
Parents: The Leightons & Houcks

Parents may seem to be a misnomer for this and subsequent chapters, but I've assigned this term even though my brother's and my parents and the parents of our wives, Dottie and Fran, are the grandparents or great grandparents of our descendants.

Young Herbert Cale Leighton

Herbert Cale Leighton was probably dyslexic. He had trouble finishing high school but later, with the help of his brother-in-law Day Mullinix, he obtained a high school diploma. In his early years he helped his father in the grocery store and in the sawmill. When he got a driver's license he worked as a chauffer for a well-to-do lady who summered in Mt. Lake Park. He also had a brief stint working in a men's clothing store in Clarksburg, West Virginia.

Leona Ronelva Houck, the daughter of **Frederick and Anna Houck,** was born September 12, 1899 in Streator, Illinois. While still in high school in Bellaire, Ohio she worked weekends in a 5 and 10 cent store in Wheeling, West Virginia. Later she worked in a millenary store that was owned by a widow. After she graduated from Bellaire High School she enrolled at the State Normal School attached to Ohio University in Athens, Ohio.

Leona Houck at Gym Class, Ohio University:
2nd from Left, 2nd Row

After completing that two year course, she began teaching in Ohio, first at a two room school house at Deep Run in Yorkville. Only two teachers at Deep Run: **Leona** taught the first and second grades and the principal taught grades three through five. To be closer to the school she and her sister **Myrdith** stayed in a rooming house.

Leona Houck with school children

Later she taught at the Rosehill School in Rockhill. When the family moved to Fairmont, West Virginia, **Leona** moved with them and taught in the Jayenne Road School in Fairmont, another two room school.

While teaching in Fairmont, **Leona** befriended a girl named **Mabel Simpson** who developed a "spot" on her lungs and was advised to go to a mountainous climate to improve her health. As a result, **Mabel** went to Mt. Lake Park, Maryland where she stayed in Hamilton Hall. During her summer vacation, **Leona** and her sister, **Myrdith** accompanied Mabel's sister on a trip to join **Mabel** in Hamilton Hall.

Hamilton Hall

Hamilton Hall was owned by the Chance family and **Leona** became friends with **Louise Chance.** Louise's brother, **Ed Chance** was a good friend of **Herbert Cale Leighton** so that's how **Leona** and **H.C. Leighton** met. They began dating and corresponding and soon became engaged. They were married on June 7, 1924.

Young Leona Houck Leighton

Living in Mt. Lake Park, **Leona** underwent three pregnancies. Unfortunately the first was a stillborn male, but the next two were successful. **Herbert Houck Leighton** was born at home on May 21, 1929. There was no hospital available nearby so Dr. McComas came to the house to perform the delivery. Two years later **Richard Frederick Leighton** was born on February 27, 1931, again at the Leighton home.

Leona, Baby Richard & Herbert Houck Leighton

The Leighton boys' father looked for more professional opportunities, independent of his father. He embarked on a partnership with **Albert White,** running a store in Loch Lynn. Then during the Hoover administration he was appointed Postmaster for Mt. Lake Park.

Not long into this position, he saw a professional opportunity in the funeral business since at that time there was only one funeral home in the county. He enrolled in the Cincinnati College of Embalming. Located at Cincinnati General Hospital, it was the oldest school of its kind in the country. To his children he became known as "our Daddy from Cincinnati."

While he was in Cincinnati **Leona** ran the post office with the help of **Mrs. Bell,** a widow who needed employment. Each month Herbert C. would return on the train to fill out reports and forms for the government. Leona and Mrs. Bell feared that the government would find out that he wasn't present full-time, but that didn't happen. With the election of FDR in 1932, this arrangement came to an end.

The Leighton family endured some hard winters in their Mt. Lake Park home which was heated with a coal stove. On cold nights the parents heated bricks and placed them under mattresses to ward off the chill. An abundance of snow was good, however, for making snowmen in the yard.

Richard, Herbert Leighton and Snowman

When **H.C. Leighton** completed his two year course in Cincinnati, he returned home but there was no site in Mt. Lake Park that was adequate to house his funeral business. As a result, he purchased a property in nearby Oakland and had a house built there. When the house was completed in 1936, the family moved in. My brother, **Herbert Houck Leighton,** known as Herbie, had completed the first grade at Mt. Lake Park but following the move he and I enrolled in Oakland Elementary School. There was no kindergarten available.

Leona kept in close touch with her sisters and mother, exchanging letters throughout the year. Summers were for visiting since Fairmont was only 83 miles from Oakland, it was an easy drive through rural West Virginia though no interstate was available then. Even so, driving up and down the hills called for frequent stops due to the boys' motion sickness. Once there, my brother and I found lots of play space among the four families of relatives. We liked to think we were helping with yard work, keeping the bird baths replenished.

Herbert Houck and Richard Leighton, doing yard work

From infancy on, Herbie's hair was brown while I had blonde curls. With the move to Oakland and shorn of my curls, I relieved my anxiety by clutching my constant companion, my teddy bear even more tightly.

Herbert Houck and & Richard Leighton with teddy bear

Busing to school was not a consideration for the Leighton boys. We could easily walk to both the elementary school and the high school.

Winter wear for us consisted of knickers, high top boots, warm coats and soft helmets with ear flaps. On sunny days the new fallen snow reflected a blinding light but sunglasses were not part of our costumes.

School work occupied much of the Leighton boys' days but there was still time to participate in operettas and to aid the war effort by knitting squares that could be sewn into larger quilts. Having attained the 6th and 7th grades in their eleven year school system (no junior high), we took on additional responsibilities in the junior safety patrol. Sponsored by the American Automobile Association, the patrolmen (then all boys) were issued white Sam Browne belts and promoted school safety by ushering fellow classmates across busy streets near the school.

Richard Leighton with junior patrol badge

In Garrett County summer vacations from school meant time to take advantage of nearby Deep Creek Lake with swimming lessons and picnic outings. Herbie's teenage growth spurt left not only me behind, but his fellow classmates as well.

Left to Right: Richard and 6th:
Herbert Houck at Deep Creek Lake

Leona prescribed piano lessons for the Leighton boys. Soon shunned by **Herbie** for other extracurricular activities, I stuck with it. Practice at home meant playing in the room where departed guests were exhibited in their caskets so my notes fell on deaf ears. Recitals were always traumatic events but the weekly lessons and practicing continued even through high school.

Richard Leighton at piano

H.C. Leighton was a joiner. He was a founding member of the Oakland Lions Club and later became its president. He belonged to a men's club called "The Owls." Members of that club played the card game, 500. He joined organizations that met in lodges, like the Masons, Knights of Pythias and Odd Fellows. He became a Rotarian as well. He and **Leona** sang in the Methodist Church choir. In their teenage years the Leighton boys joined our parents in the choir.

The lumber mill provided employment opportunities for the Leighton boys since there were always jobs to be done there like sweeping up shavings from the planing of boards.

With **H.C. Leighton** working two jobs, **Leona** assumed most of the household chores. Before the advent of modern washing machines and dryers, she pursued a basic laundry system, running clothes through a ringer and hanging them out to dry on clotheslines. To help with this laborious house work, **Leona** had a part-time helper. She also employed a high school student, **Goldie Shreve,** to help take care of the children. **H.C. Leighton** became dependent on Leona's school teacher background for his paperwork. She checked over his work for spelling and his figures for mathematical correctness.

My dad bought a lot on Deep Creek Lake. Initially he added a picnic table and an outhouse, then a boat house as well. A dock, supported by steel barrels, could be deployed in summer and retracted in winter. When the adjoining lot which had a cabin became available he purchased it as well. The lake site became a favorite spot for outings with family and friends.

After his father's death, **H.C. Leighton** sold the lumber business so he could concentrate his efforts as a funeral director. He continued to manage the funeral business until the late 1950s when, after a series of heart attacks, he was forced to retire and sell the business. When he developed pancreatic cancer, despite surgery and chemotherapy he died on May 19, 1967.

Leona continued to live in the house that had housed the funeral home. She had always been active in the Order of the Eastern Star, an offshoot of the Masons. Eventually she was recognized with a 50 year Service Award.

Leona Leighton at Eastern Star recognition dinner

She was looked after by her son, **Herbert** and his family. **Herb** had moved back to Oakland to establish a medical practice. In her later years **Leona** developed dementia so living alone was difficult.

Older Leona Leighton

In order to help her with daily activities, in her last year her grandson, **Vernon** lived with her. Fortunately, her death on December 10, 1985 was a sudden death.

CHAPTER 13
Parents: The Brocks and Chapins

Walter Burritt Brock was born on November 4, 1892, he was the son of **Fenelon Barker Brock** and **Lillian Burritt Brock**. Originally, the Brock family had lived in Maine. As mentioned in Chapter 10, Fenelon was a patent attorney in Washington, D.C. Walter married **Mabel Louise Chapin.** Born on August 2, 1899, she was the only child of **Alvin and Grace Lewis Chapin.** She spent a great deal of time on her great grandfather's (Sobieski Chapin's) farm in Virginia.

Grace, Mabel and Alvin Chapin

Walter Brock became a Presbyterian minister and the family traveled to various churches, the last one being in Oakland,

Maryland. Walter and Mabel had six children in order of birth: **Marian, Edith, Alvin, Richard, Lawrence and Dorothy (Dottie).**

First of the Brock children, **Marian Estelle** was born on May 31, 1916 in the state of New York. On September 1, 1939 she married **Robert Gamble See** in Mt. Lake Park, Maryland. He was born on March 16, 1910 in Baltimore, Maryland. Initially **Robert** was a mathematics teacher but he spent most of his career working as a tool designer for Fairchild Aircraft in Hagerstown, Maryland. He died on January 17, 1991 in Gainesville, Florida. After **Marian** raised her ten children, she became a school librarian. She died at the age of 94 on April 16, 2011 in Baltimore.

Marian and Robert See with two of their ten children:
Elizabeth and Lawrence

Edith Brock was a librarian and became the head librarian at the Ruth Enlow Library in Oakland MD.

Edith Brock

Alvin Brock served in the 29th Division of the U.S. Army during World War II. His Maryland division landed the day after D-Day and saw heavy fighting across France. Stationed north of the Ardennes on the Western Front, he was killed on November 17, 1944.

Alvin Brock

Richard Brock also served in the U.S. Army during World War II. Working on troop transports, he operated radar equipment. As his sister **Dottie** later said, "He was in the Army, but never set foot on shore."

Richard Brock

Larry Brock was skilled at engineering. During World War II he worked stateside on military technology. His sister **Dottie** remarked that "He was in the Navy, but he never set foot on a ship." After the war he worked at the University of Florida as technical staff, supporting science faculty. He also worked for an optician. **Larry** was an inventor and was awarded multiple patents.

Larry Brock

Dottie Brock was born March 19, 1930.

Dottie Brock as a child

In their mid-40s, Walter and **Mabel** divorced. **Mabel** weathered the divorce because she had sheltered her investments in a trust that Walter could not touch. It's possible that Walter's split from their marriage was due to mental illness. After the divorce he struggled to start a new career and latched onto wild ideas like explaining world history through an interpretation of the Bible. He remarried but his second wife left him after bearing another two children.

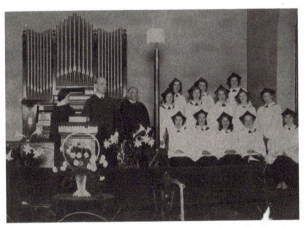

Walter Brock on the Left with church choir

Mabel Brock lived the rest of her life in Mt. Lake Park, Maryland and died on May 29, 1979. Walter died on December 16, 1980.

Older Mabel Brock

CHAPTER 14
Parents: The Scaggs and Connells

Melvin E. Scaggs, the son of **Arthur and Bessie Hines Scaggs**, was born on January 6, 1907. **Melvin** was a farmer and a painting contractor.

Young Melvin Scaggs

Myrtle Marian Connell, the daughter of **James and Elsie Connell,** was born on October 8, 1911.

Very Young Myrtle Connell

Young Myrtle Connell

Melvin Scaggs and **Myrtle Connell** married on November 9, 1930.

Young Melvin and Myrtle Scaggs

Melvin and Myrtle had five children: **Doris Marian, Frances Virginia, James Elwood**, (known as Elwood), **Mary Ellen and David Lee Scaggs**.

Doris, holding Mary Ellen Scaggs

*Left to right, 1st row: David, Elwood and Mary Ellen Scaggs,
2nd row: Doris and Frances Scaggs*

Young Frances Scaggs

Young Elwood Scaggs

The Scaggs had a large garden and they kept animals on their farm: ponies for the children to ride, cows, sheep and chickens.

David & Mary Ellen Scaggs with their pony

Melvin usually had an assistant in his painting business and the two of them did house painting in the Washington area. He was very active in Emmanuel Methodist Church in Scaggsville. He was a teacher and superintendant in the church school, a choir member and a trustee.

The Scaggs family hosted frequent dinner gatherings at their house, located in Scaggsville. Family members who gathered there included Myrtle's sisters, **Clara Connell Harris** and **Lillian Connell Milstead** with their spouses and children, as well as Myrtle's aunts: **Bertha Smith** and **Myrtle Cross.**

Left to right: Clara Harris, Melvin Scaggs, James Connell, Guy Harris, Elsie Connell, Myrtle Cross, David Scaggs, James Ritter, Keith Ritter and Mary Ellen Scaggs. Partially hidden: Doris Ritter, Myrtle Scaggs, Frances Leighton, Elwood and Patsy Scaggs

In later years family gatherings included sons-in-law and daughters-in-law as well as grandchildren.

Left to right, 1st row: Richard, Frances, Dottie and Herbert Leighton. 2nd row: James and Doris Ritter

Left to right: Kim Leighton, Jimmy Scaggs,
Diane and Keith Ritter

In1980 **Melvin** and **Myrtle** celebrated their 50th wedding anniversary.

Melvin and Myrtle Scaggs' 50th wedding anniversary

Left to right: Doris Ritter, Frances Leighton, Myrtle, Elwood, Melvin and David Scaggs, Mary Ellen Kane

Like her husband, **Myrtle** was quite active in Emmanuel Methodist Church. She was president of the Women's Society, a youth counselor and a kindergarten teacher. She also served as a delegate to the annual Methodist conference. In the community she was a member of the 5th District Planning Group, helped with local 4-H clubs and at PTA functions.

Myrtle developed breast cancer and died on January 6, 1987. **Melvin** lived another ten months and died on November 12, 1987 of heart disease. Subsequently their house was demolished to make way for the partitioning of lots for a new housing development.

CHAPTER 15
Contemporaries: The Leightons and Brocks

Herbert Houck Leighton met **Dorothy (Dottie) Louise Brock** when they were classmates at Oakland High School. He lived in Oakland and she lived with her mother in Mt. Lake Park. **Dottie** was the youngest of six children. After high school graduation, **Herb** went to Western Maryland College in Westminster, Maryland as a pre-med major and **Dottie** went to Shenandoah College in Dayton, Virginia as a voice major. Now Shenandoah is a university, moved to Winchester, Virginia. **Dottie** and **Herb** both had beautiful singing voices.

Young Dottie Brock

After three years of college Herb was accepted at the University of Maryland School of Medicine where he graduated in 1953. Later Western Maryland granted him a Bachelor of Arts degree.

Young Herb Leighton

Young Dottie Brock

In June of 1953 Herb and Dottie married at the Methodist Church in Mt. Lake Park, Maryland.

Herb Leighton and Dottie Brock wedding
1st row: Ruth Weirich, Edith Brock, Dottie Brock, Herbert and Richard Leighton. 2nd row: Minister, Edward Stephenson, Lawrence (Larry) and Richard Brock

Herb completed a year of general internship and started a residency in obstetrics and gynecology at the University Hospital in Baltimore. During this time **Dottie** taught school in Baltimore. They joined the Mt. Vernon Place United Methodist Church where they both sang in the choir and were occasional soloists.

After eight months of residency, **Herb** was drafted into the U.S. Army. He was stationed at Fort Eustis, Newport News, Virginia. With his residency background, he became the post's obstetrician and gained valuable experience in delivering babies that became the foundation of his subsequent practice.

Captain Herbert Leighton

After two years in the Army, **Herb** was discharged. He and **Dottie** returned to Oakland, Maryland where he purchased the practice of Dr. Lusby who moved to an out-of-state location. This was a good time to begin a medical practice in Oakland because, with the help of a large grant from a local resident, a new hospital had just been completed in 1950. Now designated the **Garrett Regional Medical Center** and affiliated with West Virginia University, this facility serves the medical care needs of Garrett County and of nearby communities in West Virginia and Pennsylvania.

Garrett Regional Medical Center

Herb and Dottie had four children: **Barbara Louise, Catherine (Cathy), Ann and Herbert Vernon II (Vernon).**

Left to right: Herb, Barbara and Dottie Leighton

Left to right, 1st row: Vernon and Ann.
2nd row: Cathy and Barbara Leighton

Herb's office provided a family practice but he soon had the largest obstetrical practice in town. Over his 40 years in practice, he delivered some 6500 babies.

Herb Leighton with a baby he delivered

Always a lone practitioner, he never took in a partner but he often had back-up from other practitioners in Oakland. In his later years, he took   on the job of being Coroner for Garrett County.

Older Herb Leighton

Dottie put her musical talents to good use by directing the choir at St. Paul's Methodist Church in Oakland. In those church services she was frequently a soloist or she and Herb sang duets. Recordings were made of these choral events that are still shared by family members.

Dottie liked to travel and **Herb** didn't. She made many trips, accompanied by her female friends while **Herb** preferred to stay at home. They made one trip together to Germany where their son **Vernon** was spending a college experience. In retirement, **Herb** did accompany **Dottie** to a Hilton Head timeshare which gave them a chance to visit **Fran** and me in Savannah.

Dottie and Herb Leighton in Savannah

In her early married life **Dottie** had a cerebral hemorrhage due to a ruptured intracranial aneurysm. Fortunately the aneurysm was repaired by a neurosurgeon in Baltimore. The occurrence of these aneurysms was a genetic defect in the Brock family since Dottie's sister **Marian Brock See** underwent a similar procedure. In the year 2000 another aneurysm ruptured, rendering **Dottie** unconscious. Flown to Morgantown, she underwent another surgical repair. This time the procedure didn't relieve the damage and on March 9, 2000 she died. **Herb** lived on in their Oakland house, supported by his daughters, **Ann** and later, **Barbara.**

Crippled by a stroke that left him paralyzed on one side, **Herb** became confined to a nursing home where he spent the last three years of his life, eventually succumbing. He was buried with military honors in the Oakland cemetery, next to Dottie's grave.

CHAPTER 16
Contemporaries: The Leightons and Scaggs

In my last year of high school my spinal curvature (scoliosis) became more symptomatic, resulting in my undergoing surgery: a graft from my left tibia into the lumbar spine. As a result, I missed my high school graduation. Determined to continue my education, like my brother, **Herb,** I entered Western Maryland College (WMC). Confined to a back brace for nine months, for my first year I roomed with **Herb.**

In my second year of college I met the love of my life, **Frances Virginia Scaggs.** Born on November 9, 1932 in Howard County, **Fran** entered WMC on a teaching scholarship, meaning that she was obligated to teach school in Maryland following her graduation.

Like **Herb,** I finished college in three years but I earned my degree before medical school by going to summer school, first to West Virginia University, then to WMC. **Fran** and I continued dating while I was rooming with **Herb** in Baltimore during my first two years at the University of Maryland Medical School.

Frances and Doris Scaggs at Western Maryland College

Richard Leighton and Frances Scaggs

Following Fran's graduation from WMC in 1953, we both worked that summer in Baltimore, **Fran** at the State Health Department lab and I as a scrub nurse at South Baltimore General Hospital.

Frances Scaggs and Richard Leighton at Fran's graduation

In the Fall of that year **Fran** had secured a job teaching math and science at Catonsville Jr. High School. On August 23rd, we were married. The ceremony was held at Baker Chapel and the reception at McDaniel Hall, both on the WMC campus.

Left to right: Herbert Leighton, Mary Ellen Scaggs,
Doris Ritter, Melvin Scaggs, Frances and Richard Leighton,
Roland Layton, Robert Barnett, Robert Fraser

*Left to right: Melvin and Myrtle Scaggs, Frances, Richard,
Leona and Herbert C. Leighton*

The summer after the wedding was spent at a camp in Hartford County, Maryland, sponsored by the Childrens Fresh Air Society of Baltimore for underprivileged children. I was the camp doctor and **Fran** handled the laundry.

Frances and Richard Leighton at the dispensary

Each child was presented with a new set of clothes that had to be laundered each week. My office and our living quarters were in a Dispensary building. This was a segregated experience, not unusual in Maryland in 1954. In retrospect I hope there was a similar experience for black kids.

Medical school was difficult, not because the material was difficult to master but because there was so much to learn. Today's students have even more to learn since there is now a plethora of drugs that were not available in the 1950s, but now they can quickly look them up on the internet.

Finally graduation and the match came. I had hoped for a Navy internship but my scoliosis precluded that so I settled for a year of training at the University Hospital in Baltimore.

Richard and Frances Leighton
at the medical school graduation

At that time there was a doctor draft, part of the larger Selective Service System. I was obligated to two years of military service. The Navy flight surgeon program appealed to me, requiring an extra six months. After the six months training in Pensacola, I was fortunate to get a position with Aerborne Early Warning Squadron One (VW-1), initially based in Hawaii and later on Guam. It was in the Naval Hospital on Guam that **Kimberly Ann** was born.

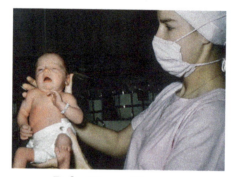

Baby Kim with nurse

Richard, holding Baby Kim and Frances Leighton, leaving Guam

Following my discharge from the Navy I had a six month interval before my residency in internal medicine began at Ohio State so I joined brother Herb's practice in Oakland. The residency was followed by a two-year fellowship in cardiology and during that time **Brian Richard** was born.

Kim and Brian Leighton in Columbus, Ohio

Following completion of my training, we moved to St. Petersburg, Florida, a stay I initially planned for a lifetime but it lasted just one year. During that year we had a house built on Tampa Bay, a concrete block house with a simulated sandstone finish, blown onto the concrete surface.

House in St. Petersburg, Florida

After a year of practice, I found I missed the academic life with opportunities to teach and to do clinical research. When I was offered the possibility of returning to Ohio State as a junior faculty member, I quickly accepted the position.

Soon after we returned to Columbus, **Frederick Howard** (Fred) was born, completing our family.

Baby Fred

We lived in Upper Arlington, a suburb of Columbus that was well known for its excellent school system.

Left to right: Brian, Frances, Fred and Kim Leighton with Missy

The years at Ohio State enabled me to obtain an appointment as the first Chief of Cardiology at the new Medical College of Ohio at Toledo. Probably the most rewarding time of my life, I was able to recruit faculty and start up new facilities: a Heart Station with echocardiography and nuclear cardiology, a CCU and a catheterization lab.

Our first home was a 3-story house on Orchard Road in Ottawa Hills, a suburb of Toledo with an excellent school system. It was there that we survived the great blizzard of 1978.

Left to right: Kim, Brian and Fred Leighton
at Orchard Road house

The cardiology facilities were added to the old Lucas County General Hospital but in 1979 we moved to a new hospital, part of the campus plan created by the renowned architect, **Minoru Yamasaki.** The move expanded our intensive care bed units with an adjacent procedure room.

MCO Hospital

With the children grown and off to college, in 1986 we moved to a unique solar house on the Maumee River, across from Waterville on River Road. Heated by a heat pump and a wood-burning stove, the double-paned windows could be filled with Styrofoam pellets for insulation.

Solar House on River Road

CHAPTER 17
Children of Herb and Dottie

Barbara completed college at Princeton University and medical school at Johns Hopkins. In 1978 she married **Will Dowling.**

Barbara Leighton

They had one daughter, **Rachel Dorothy Dowling.**

Rachel Dowling as a child

Barbara became an obstetrical anesthesiologist, first working in Philadelphia and later in New York. After she and **Will** divorced, she accepted a position at Washington University Medical School in St. Louis where she was chief of the obstetrical anesthesiology division. In St. Louis she met **Mark Salsgiver** who she eventually married. **Barbara** made several trips to Africa where she headed a team that provided medical services to the underserved people.

After **Herb** had his stroke, **Barbara** moved back to Oakland so she could supervise his care. In Oakland she became Chief of Anesthesiology at Garrett Regional Medical Center. After Herb's death she developed a uterine sarcoma that was treated with surgery and radiation and in June of 2020 she died at the age of 64. She was buried in the Oakland Cemetery near the graves of her parents.

Grave marker of Barbara Leighton

After **Cathy** graduated from the College of Wooster in Wooster, Ohio, she obtained her R.N. degree from Western Reserve University in Cleveland, Ohio. She married **Jeff Boulte**r, an emergency room physician and they settled in Lima, Ohio.

Cathy and Jeff Boulter

Cathy and **Jeff** had four children, all boys: **Daniel Jeffrey** (known as **Dan**) was born on February 23, 1982.

Dan Boulter as a child

Brian Richard was born on September 7, 1984.

Brian Boulter as a child

Sean Edward was born on June 22, 1987.

Sean Boulter as a child

Jason Herbert was born on September 23, 1992.

Jason Boulter as a child

Ann Leighton graduated from Oberlin College in Oberlin, Ohio.

Ann Leighton

She attended library school at the University of Illinois in Champaign-Urbana, Illinois. She returned to Oakland where she served on the staff of the Ruth Enlow Library until her retirement. After Herb had his stroke, Ann managed his properties and became very supportive in his care.

Ann and Herb Leighton

Like his sister, **Ann, Vernon** attended library school at the University of Illinois after he graduated from Bucknell University. He is one of the librarians at Winona State University in Winona, Minnesota.

Vernon married **Lauren Seline,** also a librarian.

Vernon and Lauren Leighton

Vernon and **Lauren** had two daughters: **Elizabeth** and **Jean Leighton.**

Top to bottom: Jean and Elizabeth Leighton

CHAPTER 18
Children of Richard and Frances Leighton

After graduating from Dartmouth College, **Kim** had a series of radio and television jobs in New Hampshire. There she met and married Robert Ellis. When Kim decided to go to medical school, she completed her first year at the University of Massachusetts Medical School in Wooster. With the breakup of that marriage and the birth of **Frances Myrtle,** she moved back to Toledo to finish medical school at the Medical College of Ohio (MCO). **Fran** and I became part of Kim's support in raising young **Frances.**

Fran reading to young Frances

In 1990 I was appointed Vice President of Academic Affairs and Dean of the School of Medicine at the Medical College of Ohio. With those titles I was privileged to hood **Kim** at her graduation from medical school.

Dean Richard hooding Kim Leighton

In Toledo **Kim** met and married **Clint Wolboldt,** also an MCO graduate. They were married by a ship's captain and young **Frances** was in attendance.

Left to right: Ship's captain, Kim and Frances Leighton,
Clint Wolboldt

Clint was an Army officer so they moved to Fort Bragg, N.C., where **Clint** completed his residency and **Kim** her internship. He completed his Army service at Fort Sill in Lawton, Oklahoma.

Then they practiced in two small towns in Texas before settling in Lubbock where **Clint** worked in an urgent care center. **Kim** obtained a Masters of Public Health degree and became Director of the Health Department in Lubbock.

Retirement and a move to Savannah for **Fran** and me provided more time for family get-togethers, both at the outer banks of North Carolina and in Maryland.

Left to right: Elwood Scaggs, Mary Ellen Kane, Frances Leighton, Doris Ritter, David Scaggs

Brian became a copy editor at the Philadelphia Inquirer. He started a long-term relationship with **Christina (Tina) Kluetmeier** When **Tina** spent a year in the Peace Corps in Russia, teaching English, **Brian** joined her for a Russian wedding, followed by a round-the-world trip through Russia, China and across the Pacific. They returned to Philadelphia where **Brian** became a senior editor with the Inquirer.

Brian Leighton and Tina Kluetmeier
with Russian friends

Brian and **Tina** soon added two children to the family: **Abigail Rose (Abby)** and **William Henry**, known as **Henry.**

Young Abby Leighton

Young Henry Leighton

After a series of computer related jobs in New York, **Fred** moved to Savannah where he obtained a Masters degree from the Savannah College of Art and Design. Following jobs teaching computer science in North Carolina and at Bowling Green State University in Ohio, he obtained another Masters degree from Georgia Tech in Atlanta. After teaching there a year, he obtained a faculty appointment at a branch of the University of Wisconsin in Whitewater.

In 2003 **Fran** and I celebrated our 50th wedding anniversary with a family week on Tybee Island and photographs in Forsyth Park, Savannah.

Left to right: Richard and Fran Leighton, Tina Kluetmeier holding Baby Henry, Brian holding Abby, Fred Leighton, Kim and Clint Wolboldt, Frances Leighton)

After a year-long battle with malignant melanoma, Fran died. Her remains were placed at the Skidaway Island Methodist Church's memorial garden, surrounded by flowers she would have loved.

Placement of Fran's remains in the Memorial Garden
at the Skidaway Island Methodist Church

With both my brother and me widowed, we kept in touch by phone and on rare occasions when I traveled to Garrett County, we got together in person.

Herb and Richard Leighton

CHAPTER 19
Grandchildren and Great Grandchildren of Herb and Dottie Leighton

I've combined the grandchildren and great grandchildren since Herb once told me that "all my grandchildren are great."

Barbara's daughter, **Rachel,** graduated from Stanford University. Based in Munich, Germany she's established a company, originally named Equalicert, now named Equal Time, that sells assessments to companies to measure diversity of their workplace and an inclusive culture.

Rachel Dowling

Cathy's son **Daniel Boulter** married **Kimberly Rose Kirkwood.**

Dan graduated from medical school at Ohio State University. He completed his training in neuroradiology at Massachusetts General Hospital in Boston. Subsequently he returned to Ohio State where he is now an Associate Professor and Medical and Clinical Director of MRI and MR in the Department of Radiology.

Dan Boulter

Dan and **Kim** have two sons. **Aiden Richard** was born on January 22, 2013.

Aiden Boulter

Owen Daniel was born on September 15, 2014.

Owen Boulter

Brian Boulter received a Masters degree in Accounting and Management Information Systems. He first worked in Columbus, Ohio but now he is Vice President of Growth & Development for 42 North Dental which is a dental practice management company for a private equity firm in Boston. He lives with his wife and family in Boxford, Massachusetts.

Brian Boulter

Brian married Laura Lee Snyder and they have two children. A son, **Wesley Richard, was** born on November 28, 2018.

Wesley Boulter

A daughter, **Hayden Joyce,** was born on October 7, 2020.

Hayden Boulter

Sean Boulter obtained a bachelor's degree in computer science at Bowling Green State University. He now manages software development teams and is a lead software developer at the Xngage company in Cleveland, Ohio.

Sean Boulter

Like his brother, **Brian, Jason Boulter** also obtained a Masters degree from Ohio State University in Accounting and Management Information Systems. He married Heidi Dang and they now live in Round Rock, Texas where Jason is a Global Partner Strategy Manager for Supply Planning, working for the Meta company, formerly Facebook.

Jason Boulter

Vernon's daughter **Elizabeth** graduated from Northland College in Ashland, Wisconsin. She obtained a master's degree and became a biologist. She married Mark Shimpf. Initially she worked in a test lab for a company that makes spices in Winona, Minnesota. Now she has a new job in a biological laboratory at the University of Wisconsin at La Crosse.

Elizabeth Leighton

Vernon's daughter **Jean** graduated from Haverford College. After college she worked for the law firm, Dorsey and Whitney in Minneapolis. Now she is enrolled in an MBA degree program at the University of Minnesota.

Jean Leighton

CHAPTER 20
Grandchildren and Great Grandchildren of Richard and Frances Leighton

With Kim's family in Texas and Brian's in Philadelphia, the grandchildren also had few occasions to get together, but they did pose for a photo after **Frances'** graduation from Baylor University.

Left to right: Abby, Henry and Frances Leighton

Another graduation was celebrated when Fran graduated from law school and joined a law practice.

*Left to right: Kim Woldboldt,
Frances Leighton, Clint Wolboldt*

During the last thirteen years, Dr. Sylvia Fields has become my partner and companion, enriching my life by her presence.

Sylvia Fields

In 2011, along with my friend, Dr. Tom Clark, we celebrated our 80th birthdays at a party held at the Telfair Museum in Savannah. Fortunately, most members of both families were able to attend.

Left to right: Frances and Abby Leighton,
Kim Wolboldt, Brian Leighton

My grandchildren are now grown and moving on. **Abby** and **Henry** both graduated from Masterman High School in Philadelphia. **Abby** is now a senior at Yale University and **Henry** is a first year student at Wesleyan University in Middletown, CT.

Abby and Henry Leighton

In 2020 Fran married Mark Rothwell, a wedding I missed.

Fran and Mark Rothwell

Fran and Mark are now the proud parents of **Layla,** my first and only great grandchild. I got to see **Layla** when she was just nine months old. Now, a year later she's walking and talking so I need to pay another visit.

Layla Rothwell

EPILOGUE

I hope this picture book will be of value to the surviving family members and in reading it, they will feel better connected. Although the younger generation of Layla, Aiden, Owen, Wesley and Hayden may not have known their great grandparents, let alone previous generations, perhaps they will be inspired to continue the effort.

INDEX

REFERENCES

1. Staley H.A.H. 2003. To Escape into Dreams. Moncure NC. Metallo House Publishers.

2. Staley H.A.H. 2011. Paper & Stone: A Leighton History in England & the United States. Moncure NC. Metallo House Publishers.

3. Sisler J.C. 1973. Christopher Cale's Family of Preston County, West Virginia, 1741-1973. Parsons, WV. McClain Printing Company.

4. Major C. 1902. Dorothy Vernon of Haddon Hall. Norwood MA. The MacMillan Company.

5. Leighton R.F. 2019. Reflections of a Hessian. Columbus OH. Gatekeeper Press.

CPSIA information can be obtained
at www.ICGtesting.com
Printed in the USA
BVHW060800231222
654908BV00007B/575